CHOICES

A Christ-centered path to
Hope and Purpose

James C. Williams

ISBN: 978-1-7324115-9-3 (Paperback)
Library of Congress Control Number: 00000000000
Front cover and book design by (Evgeniia Gurcheva).
Published by Altimese Nichole Enterprise, LLC, in the United States of America.

First printing edition 2025.

Altimese Nichole Enterprise, LLC
PO Box 2002
Savannah, GA 31402
www.coachjallday.com

This book is dedicated back to my Lord and Savior Jesus Christ, Thank you for your sacrifice

Contents

Introduction

The Power of CHOICES

*"This day I call the heavens and the earth as witnesses against you that I have set before you life and death, blessings, and curses. **Now choose life**, so that you and your children may live."*
– Deuteronomy 30:19 (NIV)

E very day we make choices—some small, some monumental—that shape who we become, how we treat others, and how closely we walk with God. The decision to love, to forgive, to press forward, to believe again—all of these are choices. And while our past might be riddled with mistakes, pain, or missed opportunities, **our future is still unwritten**. That's where hope lives.

I haven't always made the right choices. In fact, this book is born from the fire of my own failures—two divorces, seasons of doubt, and moments where I felt like I had nothing left to give. But God never left me. He didn't just restore what I lost—He **redeemed who I was**. Now, in this chapter of love and life, I walk with a deeper understanding: healing is possible, joy is available, and living on purpose is within reach—when we choose it.

This isn't a self-help book. This is a **God-helped** testimony. These seven values—**Communication, Hard Work, Organization, Integrity, Commitment, Excitement, and Sacrifice**—form the acronym CHOICES, but more important, they form a **framework for spiritual maturity** and purposeful living. They are not checkboxes of perfection, but pathways of pursuit. Rooted in Scripture and inspired by Christ, they are guiding lights for anyone who wants to live with intention and honor the God who gives us breath.

Why CHOICES Matter

Life doesn't happen to us—it flows from us.

What we say, how we act, what we pursue, and where we place our trust—it all originates from the daily decisions we make. Choices create habits. Habits shape character. Character defines legacy.

But guess what? You are not walking this road by yourself. God has always been in the business of guiding His people— through the wilderness, through the fire, through the storm. And He still is. The Holy Spirit is not just a comforter; He's a counselor. Every time you choose what is right, honorable, holy, or courageous, you echo the heart of God.

What This Book Will Do

Each chapter in this book explores one of the CHOICES values through three lenses:

1. **Biblical Truth**—Anchoring each value in Scripture to show how God models and commands it.

2. **Real-Life Reflection**—Offering personal insights, struggles, and victories from a man who's lived it and failed forward.

3. **Practical Guidance**—Simple steps and habits to walk out each value in your everyday life.

Whether you're a new believer, a seasoned Christian, a man trying to lead his family, or a woman navigating her purpose, this book is for you. It's not about being perfect. It's about being **willing**—willing to choose differently, live intentionally, and trust God fully.

A Final Thought Before We Begin

You may feel like you've already blown it—too many mistakes, too much shame, too far gone. But hear me: **God is still writing your story.** If you're still breathing, He's still building.

The question isn't *if* He will guide you.
The question is: **Will you choose Him back?**

Let's walk together through the power of CHOICES.
Let's choose life. Let's choose purpose.
Let's choose Him—again and again.

Chapter 1

Chapter 1

C – Communication: Speaking Life

"The tongue has the power of life and death, and those who love it will eat its fruit." – Proverbs 18:21 (NIV)

We live in a world overflowing with noise. Social media, text messages, podcasts, emails—everyone is speaking, but how many are communicating? And more important, how many of us are using our words to reflect the heart of Christ?

Communication is more than just talking. It is the bridge between **hearts and healing, people, and purpose**. What we say, how we say it, and who we say it to have eternal weight. Scripture tells us that our words hold the power to build or to break, to bless or to curse.

And if we're honest, many of us learned to communicate from broken places. We were taught to yell to be heard. We were taught to shut down to stay safe. We were told that emotions made us weak or that silence meant strength. But when we meet Christ, He doesn't just heal our wounds—**He teaches us a new language**.

Jesus, the Master Communicator

Jesus didn't waste words, shout over others, or manipulate. He used **stories to stir hearts**, **questions to invite reflection**, and **truth to pierce through lies**. He spoke to crowds and whispered to the hurt. And even when He was silent, His presence said enough.

When the woman caught in adultery stood ashamed before the angry mob, Jesus didn't accuse her—He *protected* her, *spoke truth*, and *restored her dignity*.

> Well, I do not condemn you either; *all I ask is that you* go and from now on, avoid the sins that plague you. – John 8:11 (The Voice)

That's the power of holy communication: it doesn't ignore the truth—it speaks it with grace and purpose.

Real Talk: My Own Journey

I've used words to wound, to win, and to walk away. I've said things in anger that I can't take back. I've also stayed silent when I should've spoken up. In my past marriages, I thought being right was more important than being relational. I thought silence equaled peace. I was wrong.

When I finally surrendered my communication to Christ, I realized that **listening is a form of love** and that my tone often spoke louder than my words.

Now, in my third marriage—built on restoration and not regret I now understand how sacred healthy and effective communication can guide all areas of a relationship. It's not just about talking. It's about connecting, and It's about making the people I love feel heard, seen, and safe.

Three Ways to Practice Christ-Centered Communication

1. Listen More Than You Speak

> *Listen, open your ears, harness your desire to speak, and don't get worked up into a rage so easily, my brothers and sisters. – James 1:19 (The Voice)*

Listening isn't passive. It's spiritual. When we truly listen, we say, *"You matter."* We create space for others to feel valued, which is exactly what Christ did every time He met someone in need.

2. Speak Life, Not Just Facts

Telling the truth is important—but how we deliver it matters. Jesus never watered down the truth, but He also never weaponized it. He wrapped truth in love and delivered it in a way that brought healing.

Ask yourself: *Will my words restore or just, correct?*

3. Invite God into Every Conversation

Pray before you speak. Ask God to guide your words—even in difficult conversations. Let the Holy Spirit be your translator when emotions rise or misunderstandings build.

What Christ-Centered Communication Produces

- **Clarity in your relationships**

- **Healing from past wounds**

- **Unity in your family**

- **Wisdom in your leadership**

- **Peace in your soul**

When your words reflect heaven, your relationships begin to look more like heaven, too.

Reflection Prompt

1. Where in your life are you speaking *more than listening*?

2. When was the last time your words brought someone peace?

3. What area of your communication needs God's healing?

Prayer

Father, help me to slow down and listen.
Teach me to speak life—not from pride, but from peace.
Let my words carry healing, and may my tone reflect Your love.
Guard my lips and guide my heart.
In every conversation, may You be glorified. Amen.

Chapter 2

Chapter 2

H – Hard Work: Faith in Action

"Whatever you do, work at it with all your heart, as working for the Lord, not for human masters."
– *Colossians 3:23 (NIV)*

We live in a culture obsessed with shortcuts. Everyone wants success, but few want to **sacrifice**. We want the mountaintop moments without the climb. But the truth is: **There is no fruit without faithfulness**. And faithfulness takes work.

Work isn't just a means of survival—it's a form of worship. From the very beginning, God created humanity to work. Adam was placed in the Garden not just to enjoy it, but to **tend and keep it**. Jesus, before He ever stepped into public ministry, worked as a carpenter. Paul, while preaching the Gospel, built tents to sustain his mission.

Hard work is not punishment. It's partnership.
God blesses what you're willing to build with Him.

The Difference Between Hustle and Holy Work

Let's be real: some of us grew up thinking that grinding 24/7 was the only way to survive. And while there's value in determination, there's also danger in striving **without God's direction**. Hustle without purpose leads to burnout. But hard work with God? It multiplies.

You know how it is, right? So many of us got this idea hammered into our heads that if you're not constantly grinding, you're basically falling behind. Like, sleep is for the weak, and your worth is tied to how many hours you clock in. And hey, there's definitely something to be said for good, old-fashioned hard work and sticking with things. That's not the issue.

But here's where it gets kinda tricky. When that hustle becomes an idol, when we're just spinning our wheels trying to prove something—to ourselves, to others, and maybe even to God—that's when we're heading straight for Burnout City. Population: us, if we're not careful. It's like running on a treadmill, going super fast but not actually getting anywhere meaningful. You end up exhausted, feeling empty and wondering what the heck it was all for.

That verse from 1 Corinthians: "Be steadfast, immovable, always abounding in the work of the Lord…" See, that "work of the Lord" bit is key. It's not just *any* work. It's work that's has a divine thumb-up, work that aligns with what God is calling you to do.

Think about it this way: Hustle, a lot of the time, is about *us*. It's about our ambition, our need for control, and our desire to be seen as successful or capable. It's often fueled by a fear of not being enough or not having enough. We're striving, pushing, and often, doing it in our own strength. And man, that strength runs out.

Holy work, though? That's different. It starts from a place of listening. It's like, "OK, God, what do *You* want me to do here? Where do *You* want me to put my energy?" It flows from a relationship, from a desire to obey and partner with God in what He's already doing. It's less about making a name for ourselves and more about making His name known.

When our work comes from that place of obedience and partnership with God, it's not just about the sweat and effort anymore. There's a different kind of energy to it, a sense that what we're doing has a bigger purpose, a lasting impact. It's like God takes our five loaves and two fish—our efforts—and does something amazing with them, something way beyond what we could do on our own. That's the multiplication factor. It's not just about avoiding burnout; it's about seeing our efforts bear real, meaningful fruit that goes beyond a paycheck or a pat on the back. It's about work that actually feeds our soul instead of draining it.

So, the challenge isn't to stop working hard. It's to shift our mindsets asking ourselves the question Are we hustling for validation, or are we working from a place of "OK, God, lead the way"? That shift can make all the difference between a life that just feels busy and a life that feels truly abundant and purposeful.

The Bible doesn't say "Be busy." It says:

> *"Be steadfast, immovable, always abounding in the work of the Lord..."* – (1 Corinthians 15:58)

The difference is this: hustle seeks validation; holy work flows from **obedience**.

My Personal Grind vs. God's Grace

For years, I worked hard to build a life that looked good on the outside. But behind the scenes, I was tired. Worn out. Running on empty. I equated my worth with what I could *do*—not who I was in Christ.

It wasn't until I failed—marriages crumbling, dreams stalling, health failing—that I realized God wasn't punishing me. He was inviting me to **work from His strength**, not my own.

Today, I am still working hard. But now it's different. I'm not proving anything. I'm simply partnering with God to live out the assignment He's given me. And that makes the work **joyful, not just heavy**.

Three Biblical Keys to Hard Work

1. Honor the Assignment You've Been Given

Stop comparing your calling. What God has asked of you is sacred—even if it doesn't feel flashy. If it's raising kids, do it well. If it's showing up faithfully at your job, do it with excellence. God sees.

> *"Do not despise these small beginnings, for the Lord rejoices to see the work begin." – Zechariah 4:10*

2. Rest Is Part of the Work

God worked six days and rested on the seventh—not because He was tired, but to set a rhythm. You don't earn rest; you obey it. True hard work includes **pausing with purpose**.

> *"In repentance and rest is your salvation, in quietness and trust is your strength..." – Isaiah 30:15*

3. Work for an Audience of One

You won't always be applauded. Sometimes, doing the right thing is lonely. But remember: Your real reward isn't a paycheck or applause. It's **pleasing God**.

> *"And whatever you do...do it for the Lord." – Colossians 3:23*

What Holy Work Produces

- **Diligence in your calling**

- **Fruitfulness in your family**

- **Endurance in hard seasons**

- **Peace in your progress**

- **Legacy through your labor**

Hard work doesn't just build success, it builds *you*. And when you work in alignment with God, **even the grind becomes grace**.

Reflection Prompt

1. Are you working from a place of striving or surrender?

2. What areas of your life require more discipline and focus?

3. What are you building today that honors God tomorrow?

Prayer

Lord, thank You for the gift of work.
Teach me to labor not in pride, but in purpose.
Strengthen my hands, renew my mind, and keep my heart pure.
Help me to honor You in every task—big or small.
May my work reflect Your glory. Amen.

Chapter 3

Chapter 3

O – Organization: Order Brings Peace

"But everything should be done in a fitting and orderly way." – 1 Corinthians 14:40 (NIV)

I f confusion breeds chaos, then **order invites peace**. Many of us long for stability—not just in our schedules, but in our souls. We pray for clarity, for breakthroughs, for things to "settle down." But what if God is waiting for *us* to create space for Him to move?

Organization isn't about perfection or control. It's about creating an environment where purpose can flourish. God is not a God of disorder. From the creation of the universe to the design of your DNA, **He moves with intentionality, structure, and alignment**. And as His children, we're invited to mirror that.

Ever notice how a mind jammed with confusion just spills into a chaotic life, while a bit of order somehow ushers in peace? A disordered mind often leads to a disordered life, while even a small amount of order can bring about peace. It's no accident. Many of us are out here craving stability—not just in our overbooked schedules, but deep down in our souls. We pray for clarity, for that breakthrough, for things to just *settle*.

But here's a thought to wrestle with: what if God's waiting on *us* to create some space for Him to work?

Now, when we talk about "organization," don't picture an impossible quest for perfection or a white-knuckled grip on control. Think of it more like this: it's about intentionally crafting an environment where real purpose can actually take root and flourish. After all, God isn't about disorder. From the cosmic dance of galaxies to the blueprint in your DNA, He operates with incredible intentionality, structure, and alignment. As His kids, we're invited to mirror that—not to be rigid, but to find a rhythm that allows His peace and purpose to flow more freely in our lives.

Jesus, the Planner with Purpose

Jesus didn't live life on accident. His days were full, yet never frantic. He withdrew when He needed rest. He arrived "at the right time" (Romans 5:6). Even the feeding of the five thousand included **organization before the miracle**—Jesus instructed the crowd to sit in groups (Mark 6:39-40). He brought order before He multiplied.

If the Son of God valued alignment and structure, shouldn't we?

OK, let's revisit this with a slightly different inflection. *What if Jesus talked directly to us today as he did when let's say Peter asked a question? Jesus why plan?*

From my vantage point, looking at how these reflections on my earthly ministry are articulated, there are certainly truths to affirm.

The concept of being a "Planner with Purpose" resonates. My life was not a sequence of arbitrary events. There was a divine blueprint, a mission underscored by prophetic foreshadowing and culminating in acts of redemption. To suggest my days were "full, yet never frantic" captures an essential truth. There was an inherent order, a divine cadence to my activities. This stemmed from a constant communion with the Father, ensuring that my actions were aligned with His greater will, rather than driven by impulsive or purely reactive pressures.

Jesus' practice of withdrawing for rest was essential for spiritual renewal and maintaining a connection with God amid the demands of ministry. His arrival "at the right time," as in Romans 5:6, signifies God's perfect timing (Kairos) in the salvation narrative. Organizing the crowd before the feeding of the five thousand demonstrates that order facilitates divine abundance. Therefore, since Jesus valued alignment and structure, we should also pursue intentional living and implement structures that promote faithfulness and fruitfulness, enabling us to co-labor with God.

Real Talk: My Own Journey

I used to think being "Spirit-led" meant flowing freely without plans. I convinced myself that structure was stifling. But truthfully, I was avoiding accountability. I let clutter pile up—

physically, emotionally, and spiritually. Missed meetings. Unpaid bills. Disconnected prayers. Unattended doctor visits. My life reflected my chaos.

When I began to submit my days to God—writing things down, creating rhythms for prayer and work, organizing my thoughts—everything changed. I wasn't just more productive; I had **peace of mind**. My home felt lighter. My prayer life became more consistent. I was more present with my family. **Order gave God room to move.**

Three Ways to Cultivate Order

1. Start with Surrender, Not Strategy

Before organizing your calendar or workspace, submit your *heart* to God. Ask: "What does heaven's order look like in this season of my life?" Let God reorder your priorities before you try to rearrange your schedule.

2. Create Systems, Not Just Lists

To-do lists are helpful, but systems create sustainability. For example:

- *Morning devotion routine*

- *Budgeting rhythm with your spouse*

- *Weekly planning time with God*

Systems make room for both structure and grace.

3. Declutter Your Space and Spirit

God often speaks clearest in stillness. Remove distractions—both physical and spiritual—to create clarity. Ask: *What's taking up space in my life that no longer serves my calling?*

What Organization Produces

- **Mental clarity** and reduced anxiety

- **Greater focus** on what truly matters

- **More consistent spiritual disciplines**

- **A sense of preparedness** for what God wants to do next

- **A peaceful environment** for your family and relationships to thrive

God's plans are orderly—and when we align with His design, peace follows.

Reflection Prompt

1. What area of your life currently feels most disorganized—and how is it affecting your peace?

2. What rhythms or systems do you need to implement to support your calling?

3. How can you invite God into your planning and structure this week?

Prayer

Lord, bring order to my chaos.
Show me how to create space for You in my time,
my home, and my heart.
Help me let go of what no longer serves my purpose.
Teach me to live intentionally and reflect Your divine
order.
Let peace flood every area that has been
disorganized or overwhelmed. In Jesus' name, amen.

Chapter 4

Chapter 4

I – Integrity: Living in the Light

"The righteous man walks in his integrity; his children are blessed after him." – Proverbs 20:7 (NKJV)

Integrity is what you do when no one is watching. ("Integrity When No One Is Watching - All Pro Dad") It's choosing truth when lying would be easier. It's honoring your word, even when it costs you. It's walking in the light—even when the shadows feel safer.

Alright, let's chat about integrity. What does it actually look like when we strip away the formal stuff and just keep it real?

That saying, "Integrity is what you do when no one is watching," is spot on, right? Think about it. It's easy to be a good person when there's an audience, when you might get kudos or a pat on the back. But true character, that solid-gold integrity, shines when you're all alone. It's like, do you return the shopping cart to the corral even if it's pouring rain and literally no one would know if you just left it? Or do you pick up that piece of trash on a deserted trail? That's the real you, the "no one is watching" you.

Then there's the part about "choosing truth when lying would be easier." Oh man, we've all been there. Telling a little white lie can seem like a quick fix, a way to dodge a difficult conversation or avoid hurting someone's feelings. But choosing honesty, even when it's super awkward or might it make things a bit more complicated in the short term? That's integrity in action. It's about facing the music, owning your stuff, and valuing truth over convenience. It's like admitting you messed up at work instead of trying to sweep it under the rug—that takes guts, and that's integrity.

Finally, "walking in the light—even when the shadows feel safer." This is about transparency and doing the right thing, even when it's scary or unpopular. The "shadows" can represent cutting corners, going along with the crowd when you know something's off, or hiding your actions because you're afraid of the consequences.

That concept of "walking in the light"? Really, it just means being straight-up with people, suggesting a life that's being lived with transparency and honesty. It's about not having things to hide, being genuine in your interaction because "light" exposes, so to walk in it means you are comfortable with your actions and motives being seen.

It's about listening to that gut feeling you have about what's cool and what's not, and going with it, no matter what everyone else is doing or saying. It usually means picking the tougher route, the one that isn't a cakewalk, simply because you know, deep down, it's the solid thing to do."

So yeah, integrity isn't always the easy route. In fact, it's often the tougher one. But it's about building a character you can be proud of, one that's consistent whether you're in the spotlight or all by your lonesome. It's about being true to your best self.

In today's world, integrity can feel optional. But for the followers of Christ, it is *non-negotiable*. God doesn't just look at what we do—He looks at why we do it. Our motives, our hidden thoughts, our private habits—they matter deeply to Him. Because before we are leaders, spouses, entrepreneurs, or friends, we are **witnesses of His character**.

Jesus, the Embodiment of Integrity

So, Jesus? He had this incredible focus. Popular opinion couldn't touch Him, and He wasn't interested in any kind of easy bargain to make things smoother. He stuck to His guns even when things got super tough. Remember when Satan tried to tempt Him out in the desert? Jesus didn't flinch or try to talk His way around it—He just fired back with Scripture and stood His ground (you can read about it in Matthew 4:1–11). And when He was basically on trial for His life? He stayed incredibly calm, choosing to keep quiet instead of defending Himself, because He knew exactly who He was and what He was about.

And here's the thing: This solid integrity He had wasn't just about following a list of rules. It came from something way deeper—He was totally aligned on the inside. What He said and did always matched up with His true identity and what He came to do. He was 100 percent committed to the Father's plan, and every single choice, every confrontation, and every act of kindness all pointed back to that one main goal. There were no hidden motives or mixed messages with Him; He was purely focused on His mission, whether it was popular or not. He was not focused on what it might cost Him personally.

Plus, His integrity wasn't just some passive, quiet quality; it was active, like a real force. It's what pushed Him to call out hypocrisy when He saw it, but always with the hope of helping people get back on the right track, not just to make them feel bad. He wasn't scared to shake things up or say the hard stuff to people in charge, even when it made things way more dangerous for Him. That kind of guts came from being secure in who He was and completely dedicated to God's big picture. So, His integrity was like the bedrock of His character *and* the fuel that powered His whole mission to change the world.

Bottom line: Jesus was the exact same guy when He was praying alone as He was when He was performing miracles for huge crowds. That kind of genuine consistency That's an amazing example for us.

Jesus was the same in private prayer as He was in public miracles. His consistency is our example.

Real Talk: My Own Journey

I'll be real with you: There were times in my life when I wore masks. Not just in front of people—in front of God. I thought if I could hide my flaws, He'd love me more. I worked hard at image management instead of heart transformation. I told half-truths, avoided accountability, and made choices I justified in the moment.

But I've learned: **secrets are heavy**, and pretending is exhausting. The more I leaned into the light of God's truth, the freer I became. Not perfect. But free. And from that freedom, integrity began to grow.

Today, I seek to live in such a way that my wife, my children, and my community don't just hear me talk about faith—they see it out in wringing out in the quiet corners of my life.

Three Ways to Live with Christlike Integrity

1. Tell the Whole Truth—First to Yourself

We can't live honestly with others if we're lying to ourselves. Ask God to show you any areas where compromise has crept in. Confession is the beginning of transformation.

> *"Search me, God, and know my heart…" – Psalm 139:23*

2. Do What You Say You'll Do

Whether it's returning a call, paying a debt, or showing up on time—keep your word. Reliability builds credibility.

> *"Let your 'Yes' be 'Yes,' and your 'No,' 'No.'" – Matthew 5:37*

3. Be Accountable to People Who Tell You the Truth

Don't walk this out alone. Invite into your life trusted voices who can call you higher and help you stay aligned with your values. God often uses community to protect your character.

What Living in the Light Produces

- **Inner peace**, because you're not hiding

- **Trust** from your family, friends, and colleagues

- **Clarity** in your decision-making

- **A powerful testimony** that draws others to Christ

- **A legacy** that outlives you

Integrity doesn't mean perfection, it means consistency. It's choosing honesty over hype and holiness over hustle.

Reflection Prompt

1. Are there any areas of your life where you're tempted to cut corners or wear a mask?

2. What's one small decision you can make today to walk in greater integrity?

3. Who in your life helps you stay accountable to your values and your faith?

Prayer

Father, I want to be the same person in private
that I am in public.

Help me live honestly—not for applause, but for
Your approval.

Show me where compromise has taken root,
and give me the strength to uproot it.

Let my life be a reflection of Your truth, Your
light, and Your love. In Jesus' name, amen.

Chapter 5

Chapter 5

C – Commitment: Faithfulness Over Feelings

"Commit your actions to the Lord, and your plans will succeed." – Proverbs 16:3 (NLT)

Commitment is the quiet decision to show up, repeatedly—even when the fire of excitement has faded, when the results are slow, and when no one is cheering. It is faithfulness in motion.

In a world obsessed with instant results and quick exits, commitment is countercultural. But commitment is the soil where deep roots grow. It's not built on fleeting emotion, but on eternal vision. It holds steady when feelings waver. That's why in the kingdom of God; **commitment is an act of worship**.

So, yeah, sticking with things isn't exactly the **most popular move** when everyone's swiping left on anything that takes more than a minute. But let's be honest, anything truly awesome you can think of—epic friendships, mad skills you've mastered, or even just that killer sourdough starter—

didn't just magically appear, right? Those deep roots we're talking about. They only get a chance to really dig in and hold strong when we decide to stay put, to keep nurturing things even when the "new and exciting" wears off. It's about choosing to pour your energy and heart into something, knowing that the real win isn't some instant success, but the kind of unshakeable strength and character that only comes from going the distance.

And look, nobody's saying it's a cakewalk. There are going to be days when your motivation packs its bags, and your "eternal vision" looks more like a blurry smudge. You'll want to bail—that's just part of being human. But commitment isn't about *feeling* pumped 24/7; it's about what you *do* when those feelings are MIA. It's that gritty, quiet decision to show up anyway, to lean into that bigger "why" even when the "how" feels a bit rubbish. That's where the real transformation happens, where you prove to yourself that you're tougher than your temporary funk and that you're serious about what you claim to value.

And here's **the amazing part**: when you start living like that, when you're the person who sees things through, it's not just your own world that gets better. People notice. That kind of steadfastness, that quiet refusal to just flake out, inspires the people around you. It's like you're silently giving them permission to aim for that too. So, that simple (but not always easy) choice to honor your word and stick to your path doesn't just build something solid in your own life; it sends out ripples. And when your everyday actions start reflecting that deep-down purpose, an "act of worship" suddenly makes a whole lot of sense—your life itself starts to point to something bigger and more lasting.

Jesus, the Faithful Finisher

So, get this: even though Jesus was God from the get-go, He didn't pull rank or cling to all His divine perks. Nope. He chose to set all that aside, stepping into the shoes of a humble servant and becoming totally human, just like us. And then, living as a man, He was all in on the path of complete obedience to God, even when that road led straight to death—and not just any death, but death on a cross (Philippians 2:6-8).

When we talk about "Jesus the Finisher," it's about so much more than just a cool title. It means He's the ultimate example of someone who truly sees things through, from start to glorious finish. We all know how easy it is to kick off new projects with a bang, full of excitement, only for that energy to fizzle when things get tough or take longer than we hoped. But Jesus wasn't about half-measures or unfinished symphonies. His entire life was a masterclass in staying the course, a perfect completion of the mission He came to accomplish. He didn't just *start* the work of salvation; He meticulously and purposefully carried it all the way to the finish line, ensuring every promise was fulfilled and every detail complete.

From the very first day He stepped into public ministry, to that final, world-changing moment when He declared, "It is finished," Jesus showed us what unwavering commitment looks like. Every single sermon He preached, every person He healed, every weary, dusty road He walked—it all pointed to this incredible, unbreakable resolve. He never once took His eyes off the prize, never wavered in His mission. And that was true even when the people closest to Him bailed, even when He was totally misunderstood, rejected, and ultimately betrayed by one of His own. What kept Him going through all that, especially knowing the immense suffering that lay ahead?

The Bible gives us a powerful insight:

"For the joy set before him, he endured the cross..." – Hebrews 12:2

Think about that "joy." It wasn't about an easy life or avoiding pain—obviously! It was the deep, profound joy of bringing us back home to God, the joy of breaking the chains of sin and death for good, the joy of opening a pathway for us to experience real, unending love and life with Him. *That* was the vision that fueled His finisher's spirit, the future He was absolutely committed to securing. He endured all of it because He was laser focused and all in committed to us, committed to the Father, and committed to completing His incredible mission of love.

That kind of commitment isn't just something to admire from a distance, it's available to every one of us, right now, through the power of the Holy Spirit working in our lives. He doesn't just show us how to finish; He empowers us to become finishers too. And here's the truly fantastic part: when Jesus declared "It is finished!" on the cross, it wasn't just the completion of His incredibly hard work; it was the ultimate "mission accomplished" that swung open the doors for us. Everything He achieved through His life, death, and resurrection—complete forgiveness, a fresh start as a new creation, direct access to God, and victory over sin's power—is now fully and freely available *to* us as believers. We don't have to strive to earn it or piece it together ourselves; we simply get to step into this amazing inheritance by faith, living out our lives on the rock-solid, perfectly completed foundation He already laid down for us.

He endured because He was committed. To us. To the Father. To the mission of love.

That kind of commitment isn't just admirable, it's available to us through the power of the Holy Spirit.

Real Talk: My Own Journey

I've made promises I didn't keep. I've started things I didn't finish. I've walked away from relationships, dreams, and disciplines when the road got hard. Commitment was a word I admired from afar but struggled to embody.

But after my second divorce, something shifted. I realized that feelings are like the weather change. But commitment is an anchor. It holds fast when everything else feels like it's drifting. In this new season of marriage, I've chosen to love beyond convenience, to forgive past comfort, and to grow even when it's uncomfortable. That's commitment. Not perfection—but presence.

Three Ways to Cultivate Faithful Commitment

1. Commit to the Process, Not Just the Outcome

Don't just commit to the goal—commit to the growth. God is often more interested in who you're becoming than in what you're achieving.

> Ask: *Am I willing to stay faithful even when progress feels slow?*

2. Guard Your Yes with Discernment

You can't commit to everything. Pray before you say yes. Then follow through with integrity.

> *"Let your yes be yes..." – Matthew 5:37*

3. Recommit as Often as Needed

Sometimes you'll stumble. But commitment isn't about never falling, it's about always getting back up. Recommit daily. Recommit prayerfully. Recommit with grace.

What Commitment Produces

- **Trustworthiness** in your relationships and leadership

- **Deeper spiritual maturity** and personal growth

- **Resilience** during long seasons and slow progress

- **Consistency** that builds momentum

- **A life marked by covenant, not convenience**

When you stay the course, you reflect the heart of a God who never gives up on His people.

Reflection Prompt

1. What's one area of your life where your commitment is being tested right now?

2. Are there any commitments you've made to God or others that need to be revisited or renewed?

3. What does it look like for you to be faithful in this season, even when it's difficult?

Prayer

Lord, thank You for being faithful to me even when I've wandered.

Teach me how to stay committed—to You, to my calling, and to the people You've entrusted to me.

Strengthen me when I feel weak. Reignite passion when I feel weary.

Help me walk in covenant, not convenience. Let my life mirror Your faithfulness. In Jesus' name, amen.

Chapter 6

Chapter 6

E – Excitement: Reclaiming Joy and Wonder

"Never be lacking in zeal, but keep your spiritual fervor, serving the Lord." – Romans 12:11 (NIV)

E xcitement isn't just an emotion, it's an outlook. In the kingdom of God, excitement is rooted in expectation. It's a heart posture that says, "God is working—and I can't wait to see what He does next." This perspective isn't reserved for grand miracles or life-altering events; it's a living, breathing anticipation that colors our perception of the everyday. It's the thrill of discovering God in the mundane, in the quiet whispers of grace, and in the unfolding of His perfect timing.

Somewhere along the way, many of us stopped living with wonder. Life got hard. Disappointments dulled our passion. Pain silenced our laughter. We mistook weariness for wisdom and settled for a predictable existence stripped of divine surprise. The vibrant hues of God's presence seemed to fade into a monochrome world. But excitement is a flame God wants to reignite—not just for Sunday mornings, but for every day. It's the renewed capacity to see His hand in the details,

His love in the small kindness, and His power in the face of our limitations.

Jesus didn't die for a life of mere survival. He came so that we might have life—and have it abundantly (John 10:10). Abundant life isn't just about provision or success, it's about living with joy, passion, and purpose, even in ordinary moments. It's the audacious belief that every sunrise holds new possibilities, every challenge is an opportunity for growth, and every interaction a chance to reflect His light. This kingdom excitement transforms routine into rhythm, obligation into opportunity, and mere existence into a vibrant, ongoing adventure with our magnificent God.

Jesus, the Bringer of Joy

Jesus' ministry was just **electric with holy wonder!** Kids practically *sprinted* to Him. Crowds followed, buzzing with expectation. The broken were healed, the hungry got fed, and the hopeless were left utterly **blown away** with awe. His presence didn't stir excitement because of flashy displays – no, **it was because He *was* hope!**

This wasn't just a band-aid for pain; it was a **total, mind-blowing reimagining of reality.** That holy wonder wasn't just some fleeting show; it was a deep, personal collision with divine love and power that **flipped their world upside down**, woke up dormant faith, and made people feel important and seen again. They weren't just impressed; they were literally transformed, pulled into a story way bigger and more thrilling than any suffering they'd known!

And get this: even staring down the cross, Jesus looked ahead with **uncontainable joy** (Hebrews 12:2). Joy was His fuel, **His ultimate high-octane boost!** He totally knew what

His sacrifice would produce—and that future joy **ignited an unstoppable strength** in His present. This was a joy born of radical obedience and an **absolute, rock-solid certainty** in the Father's awesome plan. It was the **radiant conviction** that beyond the agony lay ultimate victory—the veil ripping apart, death getting absolutely conquered, and the door swinging wide open for all of us to **truly, fully live!** His suffering was temporary, but the joy of our salvation, the very incredible fruit of His sacrifice, was eternal, providing Him with the **unwavering, exhilarating drive** to complete His mission.

Real Talk: My Own Journey

There was a time when I lost my joy. I was functioning but not living. I was busy but not passionate. I smiled in public but felt empty in private.

I asked God, "Where did my excitement go?" His answer was gentle but clear: **"You stopped dreaming with Me."**

I had let disappointments steal my expectation. But through prayer, reflection, and community, God revived something in me—not through major breakthroughs, but through simple moments. Laughing with loved ones. Praying with a brother. Watching God show up in small, unexpected ways.

Now, I don't wait for big wins to feel joy. I find it in the daily walk with Jesus—and that changes everything.

Three Ways to Reclaim Your Excitement in Christ

1. Invite God into Your Wonder Again

Pray bold prayers. Dream again with God. Get curious. Ask questions. Make room for mystery. Excitement is often born in moments when logic ends, and faith begins.

> "Call to me and I will answer you and tell you great and unsearchable things you do not know." – Jeremiah 33:3

2. Celebrate Progress, Not Just Perfection

Don't wait for the finish line to rejoice. Celebrate steps. Celebrate effort. Recognize what God is doing *now*, even if it feels small.

3. Surround Yourself with Passionate People

Passion is contagious. Find people who are on fire for God and for life. Their excitement will fuel yours. Serve with them. Laugh with them. Pray with them. Grow together.

What Holy Excitement Produces

- **Gratitude** in the present

- **Anticipation** for the future

- **Resilience** through adversity

- **Energy** for your assignment

- **A renewed relationship** with the joy of the Lord (Nehemiah 8:10)

God didn't call you to a dull life—He called you to one filled with power, purpose, and passion.

Reflection Prompt

1. When was the last time you felt truly excited about your life with God?

2. What has dulled your sense of joy or wonder recently?

3. What's one small thing you can do this week that excites your soul?

Prayer

Lord, restore my joy.
Rekindle the excitement in my heart for the life You've given me and the calling You've placed on me.
Help me live with holy wonder, to celebrate what You're doing, and to believe again in what's possible.
Let Your joy be my strength and let excitement return to every dry place in my life. In Jesus' name, amen.

Chapter 7

Chapter 7

S – Sacrifice: Love That Costs Something

"Greater love has no one than this: to lay down one's life for one's friends."" ("Why is there no greater love than to lay down your life (John 15:13 ...") – John 15:13 (NIV)

Sacrifice is the highest form of love. It's not just giving something up—it's choosing to lay something down *for someone else*. True sacrifice costs. It stretches. It surrenders comfort, convenience, and often our own desires for a greater good.

In our culture, sacrifice is often avoided. We're taught to preserve our energy, protect our time, and pursue our personal gain. But Jesus turns that upside down. In the kingdom, **giving is gaining**, and sacrifice is the pathway to both impact and intimacy with God.

You can't walk in purpose without walking through sacrifice. Whether it's your time, your pride, your plans, or your resources—**what you're willing to lay down often reveals what (or who) you truly love**.

Jesus, the Ultimate Sacrifice

The entire gospel rests on something truly incredible: a radical, earth-shattering sacrifice. Jesus gave everything—His position, His rights, His comfort, His very life—for us. He didn't just preach love; He absolutely *proved* it. He stepped into the profound brokenness of humanity, where a gaping chasm separated us from a holy God, and offered Himself as the perfect, divine bridge.

"But God demonstrates His own love for us in this: While we were still sinners, Christ died for us." – Romans 5:8 Seriously, let that sink in: Not when we had it all together, not when we earned it, but when we were at our worst, messy and miles away. *That's* when He gave His all.

Jesus wasn't forced onto the cross—He passionately, intentionally chose it. That's what makes His sacrifice so incredibly powerful. It wasn't taken from Him—it was freely, sacrificially given. And this choice, this perfect, willing offering, is what makes it the *ultimate* sacrifice. It wasn't just *a* payment; it was the *final* payment, comprehensive and complete, settling a debt no human effort could ever touch. It's the deepest, most radical expression of unconditional love the universe has ever witnessed, bridging that impossible gap between us and our Creator once and for all.

So, what does this monumental act mean for *everyone*? Even if you don't subscribe to the specific beliefs of faith, the story of Christ's sacrifice redefines what true love and selflessness look like. It speaks to the universal human experience of wrestling with imperfection, guilt, and the longing for a fresh start. It offers a profound narrative of putting another's well-being, even their eternal destiny, above one's own comfort and life. It's the grandest display of grace, challenging us all to reconsider what it means to forgive, to live with compassion, and to embrace a love that gives even when it costs everything.

And now, as His followers, we're called to carry our own cross daily (Luke 9:23). That means living lives marked by sacrificial love—not to earn grace (because it's already given!), but to powerfully reflect it. It's our excited, grateful response to the most generous gift imaginable. It's living a life that boldly declares, **"Because He gave *everything*, I can give too!"** It's choosing to love, serve, and extend grace in a broken world, believing that this same power of self-giving can bring transformation, reconciliation, and hope to everyone around us, one person, one moment at a time.

Real Talk: My Own Journey

Sacrifice used to feel like a loss to me. I thought if I gave up something, I'd be left with less. But I've learned this: **when I sacrifice with the right heart, God always fills what I emptied**.

I've sacrificed pride to say, "I'm sorry."
I've sacrificed opportunities to honor my marriage.
I've sacrificed time to mentor younger men.
And every time, I've gained more than I gave.

In my previous marriages, I confused sacrifice with silence or self-neglect. But true sacrifice isn't about losing yourself, it's about laying yourself down *in love*. In marriage I've grown to learn that sacrifice must be mutual, rooted in respect, and surrendered to God.

Three Ways to Walk in Sacrificial Love

1. Start Small, but Stay Sincere

Sacrifice doesn't always mean grand gestures. It could be giving someone your undivided attention, waking up early to pray for your family, or offering your resources when no one's looking. Small sacrifices, made consistently, build a big life of love.

2. Give Without Expecting Something Back

The purity of sacrifice is revealed when there's no applause, no payoff, and no returned favor. Real love gives, period.

> *"If you love those who love you, what reward will you get?" – Matthew 5:46*

3. Let God Fill What You Lay Down

When sacrifice leaves a space, invite God into it. He fills with peace what you gave in obedience. He never It's sacrifice go unnoticed—or unrewarded.

What Sacrificial Living Produces

- **Deeper intimacy** with Christ

- **Stronger relationships** grounded in selfless love

- **Humility** that softens pride

- **Compassion** for others' needs

- **Eternal impact** that outlives your earthly comfort

When we lay down our lives in love—in our homes, our workplaces, our churches—we live like Jesus. And *that* is the highest calling.

Reflection Prompt

1. What is God asking you to lay down in this season?

2. Have you been resisting sacrifice out of fear or pride?

3. Who in your life would be blessed by a small act of sacrificial love this week?

Prayer

Jesus, thank You for showing me what real love looks like.

You gave everything—not because You had to, but because You wanted to.

Teach me to live with the same heart.

Help me see where I need to lay down my comfort, my plans, or my pride for the sake of love.

And as I sacrifice, remind me that You always fill what I surrender. In Your name, I pray, amen.

Conclusion

Your Life, Your Legacy

"I have set before you life and death, blessings and curses. Now choose life, so that you and your children may live." – Deuteronomy 30:19 (NIV)

The road of life is paved with decisions. Some are small and seemingly insignificant. Others carry weight for generations. But no matter where you've been, no matter what you've done, or what you've lost—you can begin again. Right here. Right now.

Hope is always a choice.

This book wasn't written to impress you. It was written to remind you. To remind you that your choices matter—and they don't have to be perfect to be powerful. What matters is that you're willing. Willing to change. willing to grow and willing to walk hand in hand with God into a new beginning.

Legacy Built on CHOICES

Each of the principles in this book—**Communication, Hard Work, Organization, Integrity, Commitment, Excitement, and Sacrifice**—is a spiritual discipline. A reflection of God's character. A seed that produces fruit when tended to daily.

You may not always feel like you're making progress. But every time you choose to listen with love, work with purpose, bring order to your life, stay true to your values, show up when it's hard, rejoice in the small things, or give selflessly, you are building a legacy.

Long before you ever speak, your life is being observed, and your actions speak volumes about what you truly believe.

Let Your Choices Speak for You

You don't have to explain yourself to everyone. You don't have to prove yourself to people who don't understand your process. Let your consistency speak. Let your faithfulness testify. Let your choices honor the God who saved you.

Because the truth is, when you follow Christ-centered values, **you'll stand out**—not because you're trying to be perfect, but because you're committed to living with purpose.

What Will You Choose Now?

As we close these pages, I pray you feel empowered—not burdened. You don't need to change everything overnight. Start with one choice. One value. One prayer. One moment of obedience. And let God multiply it.

The same God who walked with Abraham, strengthened Moses, redeemed David, and restored Peter—He walks with *you*. He sees your daily decisions. He honors your surrender. He celebrates your return.

So, choose to communicate with love.
Work like its worship.
Organize with intention.
Live with integrity.
Stay committed.
Reignite your excitement.
And lay your life down in love.

Final Prayer

Father, thank You for giving me the gift of choice.
I surrender my life, my habits, and my heart to You.
Help me to live by the CHOICES that reflect Your character.
Let my life be a testimony of Your grace, Your patience, and Your power.
May my legacy not be built on perfection—but on faithfulness.
I choose You today and every day that follows. In Jesus' name, amen.

21-Day Challenge

Appendix

21-Day CHOICES Challenge

Living the Values, One Day at a Time

"But be doers of the word, and not hearers only..." – *James 1:22 (NKJV)*

Transformation doesn't happen in one big leap it happens one faithful step at a time.

This **21-day challenge** is designed to help you live out each value in the CHOICES framework with intention, reflection, and connection to Christ.

You'll focus on one core value every three days, with a daily challenge, a Scripture to reflect on, and a journal prompt to deepen the experience.

Structure

- **Days 1–3:** Communication

- **Days 4–6:** Hard Work

- **Days 7–9:** Organization

- **Days 10–12:** Integrity

- **Days 13–15:** Commitment

- **Days 16–18:** Excitement

- **Days 19–21:** Sacrifice

Days 1–3: Communication

Scripture Focus: James 1:19 – "Be quick to listen, slow to speak, and slow to become angry."

- **Day 1:** Practice active listening with one person today.
  How did it feel to listen without interrupting or responding right away?

- **Day 2:** Send an encouraging text or handwritten note to someone.
  What did their response teach you about the power of words?

- **Day 3:** Ask God to show you how to speak life more consistently.
  Where is God challenging you to speak truth in love?

Days 4–6: Hard Work

Scripture Focus: Colossians 3:23 – "Work at it with all your heart, as working for the Lord."

- **Day 4:** Choose one task you've been putting off—and do it with excellence.
  How did it feel to complete something instead of procrastinating?

- **Day 5:** Reflect on the difference between busyness and purpose.
  Where is God calling you to be more intentional in your work?

- **Day 6:** Identify how your work (paid or unpaid) honors God.
  How can you worship through your daily responsibilities?

Days 7–9: Organization

Scripture Focus: 1 Corinthians 14:40 – "Everything should be done in a fitting and orderly way."

- **Day 7:** Clean or organize one physical space in your home or work.
  How does physical order impact your mental peace?

- **Day 8:** Block time in your schedule for uninterrupted prayer or reflection.
  How does scheduling your spiritual life help protect it?

- **Day 9:** Make a list of your current priorities and commitments.
  Do they reflect God's order—or your own overload?

Days 10–12: Integrity

Scripture Focus: Psalm 25:21 – "May integrity and uprightness protect me..."

- **Day 10:** Tell the full truth today, even when it's uncomfortable.
  What happened when you chose honesty over ease?

- **Day 11:** Make amends for something you've been avoiding.
  How did that step bring peace or healing?

- **Day 12:** Reflect on any "hidden" areas of your life.
  Where is God inviting you to walk in greater transparency?

Days 13–15: Commitment

Scripture Focus: Galatians 6:9 – "Let us not become weary in doing good…"

- **Day 13:** Recommit to one discipline or goal that's been neglected.
  Why is this commitment worth fighting for?

- **Day 14:** Honor one promise you've made—no matter how small.
  What does your follow-through say to the people around you?

- **Day 15:** Identify one way to show up when it's inconvenient.
  How does faithfulness strengthen your character?

Days 16–18: Excitement

Scripture Focus: Nehemiah 8:10 – "The joy of the Lord is your strength."

- **Day 16:** Do something today that brings you pure joy.
  How can joy be an act of resistance against weariness?

- **Day 17:** Reflect on a recent win—big or small—and celebrate it.
  What does celebration teach you about God's

goodness?

- **Day 18:** Ask God to renew your sense of wonder.
  Where is God moving in your life in quiet but powerful ways?

Days 19–21: Sacrifice

Scripture Focus: Romans 12:1 – "Offer your bodies as a living sacrifice..."

- **Day 19:** Give something away that matters to you—time, energy, or a possession.
  What did that act of surrender reveal about your heart?

- **Day 20:** Serve someone who can't repay you.
  What does sacrificial love cost you—and what does it restore in you?

- **Day 21:** Pray: "Lord, what do You want me to lay down?" Then act on it.
  What freedom did you experience in obedience?

Final Reflection: Living CHOICES Daily

"Lord, I choose to walk in Your way. Let my daily decisions reflect my trust in You. Help me to live a life that honors You—one choice at a time."